THOUGHTFUL WANDERER

SHRUTI BHARDWAJ

Copyright © Shruti Bhardwaj
All Rights Reserved.

"I DEDICATE THIS BOOK TO MY
PARENTS"

Contents

Contents

FOREWORD

Thoughtful Wanderer is a collection of countless thoughts that go around in my mind on a daily basis. It is a collection of poems that I have composed by thoroughly observing, analyzing and interpreting day to day events of life, so as to share my views, feelings, thoughts and expressions with like minded personalities. Being a working professional in the field of teaching since the past 5 years, I have had the opportunity to face several challenges, gain a lot of experiences and knowledge about a wide range of topics, which I plan to share through this piece of work.

So, let's set our minds free and allow our thoughts to wander off onto new interesting journeys!

Shruti Bhardwaj

Acknowledgements

First and foremost a big thank you to God almighty for the endless showers of blessings throughout my project called **'THOUGHTFUL WANDERER'**, my debute book as an author.

The acknowledgements for **'THOUGHTFUL WANDERER'** would be absolutely incomplete without the mention of my pillars –

Mom & Dad for always being there by my side and letting me fly freely towards my dreams. They both are my constant support.

Bharti Sharma my guiding soul and the lady I adore. She is the one who actually made me whatever I am today. Thank you for your never-ending guidance, love, faith and support.

Tanubhav Sharma who brought a ray of hope in my life and made me fall in love with myself. He taught me the art of dreaming, working, achieving and made me believe in myself, my potentials and gave strength to my wings. I still remember the way you keep on sitting the whole night encouraging me to move ahead saying **"everything is ok just focus on your efforts trust yourself and don't worry about the result"**. Thank you for holding my hand in my toughest time when all my dreams were shattered.

ABOUT THE AUTHOR

SHRUTI BHARDWAJ

Shruti Bhardwaj born and brought up in Delhi is a bilingual poet is an alumna of the prestigious MCM DAV College, Panjab University. She is passionate to write poetries and articles in English & Hindi and a number of them have been published on several websites and reputed E-newspapers like 'The Times of India'. She considers writing as a creative way of teaching and also expressing. She is a voracious reader and believes that reading all genres has helped her to be a versatile writer and poet too. She contributed in many anthologies as a writer and got a chance to edit a few. Further she judged many writing contests with different organizations.

Apart from the above she is presently working as a dedicated teacher in a reputed school and running her own academy as a Spoken English Trainer by the name MILESTONE ACADEMIA wherein she is guiding students across India and some foreign countries as well through online mode.

ACHIEVEMENTS & RECOMMENDATIONS:

Published Works In The Following Anthologies:

The Teacher I Will Never Ever Forget

Mumbai Meri Jaan

Will You Be My Valentine – Book 1

The Trying Times

Paint My World Green

Women V/S We Men

No, I Am Not Okay!

Inked Thoughts

Lockdown Diaries

Love Is My Religion

Kaafi Hua (Hindi)

Khatti Mithhi Batiyan (Hindi)

The Impish Lass Requiem

Other Published Works:

Lockdown Saga – LPU Official Website, The Times of India E-Newspaper

Failure a Brick in the Castle of Success – The Times of India E-Newspaper

Lockdown: Blessing in Disguise – The Tribune

Research Paper Presentations on the following topics:

"Sustainable Development" in CHASSONG- 7TH in 2017, Panjab University, Chd. "Addiction in Youth" in an International Conference on 'OLYMPISM' in 2018 at Dev Samaj College of Education, Chd.

Edited Works:

Failure a Brick in the Castle of Success...

Let's Breakup with Stress and Fall For...

Midnight Musings

Rebirth & Emotions
The Guru (Ebook)

Acknowledgements & Proofreading Works:

No, I Am Not Okay! – An Anthology by Ms. Meena Mishra
Impish Lass – Book 2 – A Book authored by Ms. Meena Mishra
Inked Thoughts – An Anthology by Ms. Praniti Gulyani
Sixteen Drops of Ink – A Book by Ms. Praniti Gulyani
Designated as Literary Lieutenant in the 'Army of Literary Warriors' by Story Mirror

CERTIFICATE OF APPRECIATION - Presented poems in International Poets' Meet organized by R.S Mundle Dharampeth Arts & Commerce College, Nagpur.

UNIQUE ANTHOLOGY CERTIFICATE for Let's Breakup with Stress and Fall For...

CERTIFICATE OF APPRECIATION by SOF for conducting and preparing students for IEO in 2018 and 2019.

CERTIFICATE OF APPRECIATION for giving inputs and conducting EXUBERANZZA an Inter School virtual competition organized by Alliance International School in 2020.

SPORTS ACHIEVEMENTS:

Silver Medal in Chi Kwang Do – DISTRICT (August 2014)
Silver Medal in Chi Kwang Do – STATE (October 2014)

MUSINGS

I

FAILURE - A STEPPING STONE

Failure is all about a stepping stone,
Not a dead-end or a stop.
We are trained not to fail,
And if we do, it is a terrible sin.
I try to move past it and reach the end,
But everyone keeps pulling me back to the start.
They say failure is the end wall,
That I cannot turn back the clock.
Then there is a whisper in my head,
Telling me that from failure I shall ascend.
Failure is like a two-sided coin,
I can either go back or go forth.
I know that I will fall a thousand times,
But I will never stop trying.
'Don't fight it'- said the whisper,
'Accept it and see the magic happen.'
'It is from failure that you can learn,'
'You learn about the barriers that you have in your way.'
'Embrace the difficult situations,'

'They tell you how far you have come.'
Failure is all about a stepping stone,
For it is from here that you shall unlock the success of the
world.

• 4 •

II
THE DISGUIDED BENISON

Drenched in resolutions of victory?
Let the zephyr of defeat fan you,
Bask in the ephemeral pleasure of the relief,
While your life's canvas gets tainted with a different hue.
When white remains abstruse without black,
And a buoyant day, none but a sombre night can drive,
When the mighty sun has to set every day,
Can success without failure thrive?
Debacles are often the embers,
Which melt the fetters binding a pusillanimous soul,
Stoking the flames of passion and courage,
They steer you towards your coveted goal.
Bitter be the potion of trouncing,
It cures contusions with the vital experience,
No matter how distasteful it is to the tongue,
Within, it waters the seeds of resilience.
Failure isn't a matter of distress,
Never label it as a hassle,
It is indeed the quintessential brick,

That completes success's sumptuous castle.

III

FAILURE- Just a bend, not the end

Failure; a mere seven letter word,
Yet the spell of doom it casts over everyone is absurd.
From childhood we are taught failure is not an option,
Yet it stalks us through life with gumption.
For life is one long exam,
And success is not often achieved, the very first time.
We try, we fail, we learn,
That is how worth is earn.
From Walt Disney to J K Rowling, Michael Jordan to Steve Jobs,
Fail they all did, yet rose like phoenix from ashes.
Inevitable is failure, once we get into the business of life,
Depends on us whether we fall or thrive.
The thought of failing knots our stomach and cramps our heart,
The ones who succeed after failure that are called stalwarts,
Those who never give up become great,
Strength, courage and resilience become their defining trait.
The ones who fear failure never try and do not put anything at
stake,

Always scared, thinking their efforts might end up being a
mistake.
Failure provides a chance to learn and grow,
Those unable to see, miss the opportunity to glow.
Prosperity shines on those who can hold under duress,
For failure is just a brick in the castle of success.

IV
BLESSING IN DISGUISE

Dates of 'lockdown' are passing, today is 22nd April,
Everyone is in fear, there is no thrill.
Gradually tentacles of Corona are spreading,
Leading us for more days in quarantine.
God knows.....what is the plan for future?
As our mother Earth is healing her sutures.
The damage done to her is a lot,
I think, this is the only way she has sought.
Seems she needs some more days,
Her wounds are blue, deep and at bays.
Everything is done to maintain a balance,
So there is fear, turbulence and reverberence.
It's high time to set the ecosystem,
Just to halt our violent habit and fashion.
Observe ......there is no crime happening, no accidents,
The air is clean, the sky is blue transparent.
Variety of birds have migrated,
Wild life!!! On once busy roads, created.....
Wao! The nature is blossoming,

Colourful flowers, trees with new foliage shining.
You mind your business, enjoy at your place,
Be creative and innovative; don't let this golden opportunity
waste.
If saved, we are going to miss this time,
And will remember forever the peace of quarantine.
COVID -19 appears to be arms in disguise,
To bring balance, awareness and lesson of what is right.
But still......selfish human,
Won't learn any lesson and will remain inhuman.
Anyway there always lies a hope...
Everything will be normal, may we again rock!!
Humans fail to scrutinize the severity at virus outbreak...
Gradually, we are learning with our mistakes.
This failure of human being to understand the mystery...
God's plans are superb as told by the whole history.
Hopeful in future there won't be such pandemic anymore...
Mother earth have healed and taught many lessons therefore.

V
FAILURE

We failed through the times
when we learnt to learn the Rhymes
We failed through the Psalms
when we learnt to keep the calm
We failed when we lived it.
Accept and Move On they say
Failure is assimilation and fay.
Fall twice and get up thrice
Failure is getting up to be ice 'n' nice.
We failed when we lived it.
It was not about the endurance
But maybe the endearment
It was not about the idealism
but maybe the realism.
We failed when we lived it.
Immuring the pen was a failure
Foisting the Ken was a failure
Not shelling the self was a failure
Not knelling the felt was a failure
We failed when we lived it.
Tussled or Soar;
Authenticity is success

Sublimate or Roar;
Enunciation is success
We'd succeed when we live it
Writhe or Brawl;
Restitution of the soul is Success
Perversity or Morality
Acceptance of the self is Success
We'd succeed when we live it.

VI
HOPE HELPS TO SUSTAIN

It's due to NOVEL COVID -19,
We're forced to be quarantine.
Everyone locked in...
It's high time of quarantine.
But, with the few who are still out....
The chain won't break; each of us will panic and shout.
If you love humanity,
Stay at home and change the VIRUS calamity.
It's just the question of twenty one days....
Six are over; fifteen more are on their ways.
The time we all are facing won't come tomorrow,
Uncertainties...with active lend and borrow.
When we talk about male gender,
Stressful about tomorrow, but still working under.
Doing all domestic chores they have not done before,
Must have come across the hard work, females does, for sure.
This TIME when no one of us in a hurry, hoarding done, want
no more,
Leading stressful, informal life, no one knocking at the door.

Spending time together with kids,
Parents' attention, love, time….they were badly seeking it.
Keep on passing time with creativity,
Let the hidden talent show their positivity.
GOD! I pray for the world,
To give courage and remedy to cross all hurdles.

VII
VOICING THE UNVOICED

Perturbed by the situations,
We dare to take big steps,
Without any preparation we dare to leave your doorsteps,
Smiling faces with heart full of tears,
Always wearing fake smiles...
WE,
Bear Bear and Bear.
Carrying our houses on our heads,
Making your life easy,
So that you can sleep on beds,
Shocked by the setbacks that we had,
Though we are sad we make you feel glad.
In seconds you throw us like rotten sacks,
Without thinking about the little ones,
You refrain us to contact back,
Like rotten fruit's sack
You throw us outside,
Without thinking about the little ones
Crying beside.

With heavy hearts we started our journey,
look our lives are losing even its power of attorney,
With bleeding feet and heavy heart,
We are moving towards the places we reside,
Keeping our problems and health everything aside.
Harsh realities again knocked the door,
This time they entered from the back door,
With many setbacks and a lot more.
The God is angry to see our miseries,
You are busy in creating mysteries,
Our heart is aching,
You are baking,
Acting as if sinking you guys are merrily singing...
Our aching hearts are full of fear,
Feeling as if still we have a lot more to bear.
A LOT MORE TO BEAR...

* * *

Note:Dedicated to the brave COVID warriors who have played crucial and life saving roles in testing times and are still on their voyage.

VIII
STRESS OR A MESS

If you close your eyes
You will find the truth revealed
And if you don't …
All your scars would never be healed
To those who have stress,
Those engulfed in the darkness
All you need is some caress,
Otherwise you won't find success.
Those who hold the stress for longer
You're just making it more stronger.
You won't last for longer
If you make stress a life longer;
So when you are in distress
Just release the stress
Don't let it suppress;
Never let your emotions to get over
That's how you climb the stress tower.
Well, you won't have to become a Rover
You just need to gain more Power;
To get rid of stress
One should not feel depress
Because God is always there to bless

If you have any doubts, I guess;
And if you find someone stressed
Don't hesitate to motivate
Don't let him become bait;
Always remember, this feeling has to be contradicted
With pure souls and Negative thoughts evicted.

IX
Ode to Women

Women are the birth givers,
The power of the nation,
BUT
Since ages, this world was so irrational;
I always think sitting in the corner,
Why women have to bear all the tortures?
Why is she being judged at every point?
Why does she have to be in shame all the time?
Her activities are put on halt,
Why is a teasing done by a boy her fault?
I always think sitting in the corner,
Why women have to bear all the tortures?
Wearing a short skirt, she might be characterless
THEY SAY...
I am going out with a boy,
How dare she say;
Every time she is used as a device
Give some respect,
O MAN ...
She is your wife,
Holding a knife
Cooking for you to survive

Just a simple advice,
Stand by her side, to help her rise.

X
MOMIEE...

Paradigm of perfection,
My dear mom
Where are you from?
How can you bear this worldly storm...
with a smile on your face,keeping tears inside?
You always stand beside
And guide me to ride.
Mumma
You are...
Epitome of perfection,
And
I will always try become your reflection,
Yes,
You are embodiment of perfection,
Though sometimes give me false reaction,
But
Always clear my misconception,
O Mom
Where are you from?
How can you bear...
this devastating storm?
Without any fear,

You always bear,
Still for us...
You brings in cheer,
O my dear...
Whenever I fear,
You always appear,
And
Set the way clear.
With you by side
I start my ride,
Keeping fear aside,
I learnt to decide,
I promise
I will always abide
And
Be your pride.

XI

AND I FELL FOR HER AGAIN

She looks at me with a dazzling eye
That gaze gives me the love of the entire
She got the confidence full of fire
And that rock lady gets a little shy
She looks at me and every time I fell for her
Her lap is warmer than a fireplace
When she hugs me tight, the whole world I don't bother
And that cosy soul is my MOTHER
Motherly care, my essence desires for only this shade
She keeps me warm and I fell for her again
She gave me birth with lots of pain
I slip all sorrows listening her smiling stories
And that cheerful flower hides her grief behind her twinkle
glories
All of us must love our mothers otherwise it's a shame
Her heavenly love makes me fell for her again
I look in her and I see a divine
Realized she is the purest gift of God
And that rarest diamond takes a little and gives a lot

Her care is the base for me to shine
She is my inspiration and I fell for her again.

XII
MY LOVE

Wandering with an aching heart
In the search of meaning
With lacerated cuts
I shout and scream,
Carrying a brook of silent tears
In my eyes
The mind was turbulent
With overflowing ideas
Trying to excel
But,
Failing like a bad criteria
Every single day I looked out like a chirping bird,
In no time
Shooed unheard...
Shouting...
Groaning...
Peeping ...
Sleeping...
Each day, each night passed away
And,
One blissful morning
With a light of hope,

I looked out again into the world
I saw you...
Roaming with some positive vibe...
And,
One beautiful night
You became my guiding light,
Promised holding my hands,
And visited my site...
Saying
"Everything is alright"
"Come on... go on...explore...demand ...achieve"
You shouted from behind
"I am with you"
"Go ride and wide"
Sitting side by side
You taught me to drive
To deal life with gratification and pride
You always escorted from beside
Facing hurdles day and night,
You made me right!

XIII

FALL

Season of fall, pretty colors and hues
Season of scandal, birth and mortal news
Season to let go of all bitter cups
Season to embrace and fall in love
Season to walk through that foggy dawn
Season to crush leaves and laugh alone
Season to feel warmth of the sun
Season to let go of worldly bumps
Season of rebirth, of burying the past
Season to relinquish stress and relax
Season to rejuvenate as a new you
Season of happiness in my view

XIV

QU'EEL EST MOI

Carrying smile on her face
She walked in full grace
Leaving behind the retrace
She focussed on the chase
Jealous people tried to bar her freedom
But
She seldom paid attention so as to enjoy in her kingdom
A loud discouraging voice
Trying to change her choice
Refrained her to rejoice
Bombarding her with unpleasant surprise
With an aching heart
She supported herself from falling apart
Believing that every day is a new start
She always acted very smart
To give herself a kick-start
Knowing that no one would like her to be a part
Of Saying
I AM NOT OKAY !
She decided to ride her own cart
With a lacerated heart
She wept

And said
I am Okay!
Deep inside the heart she was broken and NOT OKAY!

XV
SURRENDERED SELF

A day so sad and solemn would mark; the soul would leave the
world and go
And I would witness the sorrows of my loved ones
Lamenting the departure of another, in woe
Who stands here so responsible to allow this all?
Who stands here so brave deafening to hear a man call?
Who has the might to absorb his suffering and pain
No one, alas ,when there's so much to gain
I had heard of cannibals , they live in the thickets
But little did I know I'll Face them here
Where pyres will alight amidst the once happy lands
I'll see them there smiling in saltless tears
You might have failed to recognise their dirty and treacherous
part
Growing horrendously lashing their spiteful fangs
I know not how man will heal his heart
Of how he will carry his empty selfless soul
For I see the skies still continuing to darken their clears with
soot
While the nights like serpents stealthily linger to lengthen their
deadly roots
The times are tough the loss is grave

I gave up hope of mankind to save
The world that is chained to slavery and disgrace, but
Day and night will change with their course
While the heart will silently sob in remorse
Is there something that could reverse the time
For happier moments to come and and stay as mine
Memories of the love lost will remain a song
A silent tune in my heart till I'm gone
And till then you will be a thought to cheer
As I miss u in me , a silent tear.

XVI

HOW SELFISH HAS THE HUMAN BECOME!

How selfish has the human become!
Squandering over the jewels with fuss
Pleading to nature clenched in hands a candelabrum
Now haven't they turned into Judas?
And forgotten the strength of god, Alas!
The rings of suffering of Mother Nature
Are signs of engagement of human favor
Don't be delighted, it's not a benediction
Suppressing Mother Nature's screams have become a human
addiction
The rising smoke and stubble's burning flame
Show over the years how loutish humans became
Calling for trouble, we burnt stubble
We threw ourselves as the ball
This does not seem a human trait
This craving has to be contradicted
With pure sails and negative thoughts evicted

Last time! Mother Nature blessed us with a wakeup call
Lets respond, or else the entire human empire will fall!

• 33 •

XVII

MOTHER NATURE

Mother Nature finds a way,
She renews life, death and decay
She brings the rain to save us from drought,
Shines the sun, so that leaves can sprout.
Mother Nature is a queen,
Sometimes her beauty is unseen,
Through her touch and in her hand,
She brings beauty to the land,
Mother Nature always finds her way
She gives us life, beautifies the place where we stay.

XVIII
LOCKDOWN SAGA

Lockdown... Lockdown...
Stay at home,
It's a time to pray at home,
Sit at home don't go outside,
Instead meditate and go inside,
It's a time to recreate yourself,
Think about yourself
And
Work for yourself,
Get up all don't be sad,
Take it as an opportunity
And feel glad.
Put all the negativities and the current situation on one side,
Which is not in our hands...
But,
Always stay planned,
Never let the situation go out of hand,
Take precautions and just understand,
Take a nap,
Meditate or Read,
Be with yourself,
And do good deeds,

Do whatever your hectic schedules refrain you from doing every
time,
Enjoy family time, which you get sometime,
Take this as an opportunity instead of taking it as bad times,
Trust the lord and sing his hymns.

XIX

I DARE TO WRITE

Sitting silently everyday in my backyard,
The thoughts act like a sword,
I thought that I can't do anything think my fellow young bards,
Every single word from the surroundings,
Act like a sword,
Holding me back and bombard,
Leaving behind ugly scars;
My thoughts scoffs
And...
I f...m...ble
The laugh at me whenever I stumble;
Words often swims in my head
But,
Vanishes when I feel sad,
They say I have done nothing to feel glad;
Then entered my crumpled papers and mind again in my life,
They brought me into the lime light,
They are one that made me feel bright,
And
That very night I dare to dive
In the ocean of words
To write.

XX
MY LOVE FOR YOU

Even though you are far from me,
My heart feels you near,
I feel comfort in your arms,
You take all my fear,
You encourage me to explore and bear
Saying...
For I am with you ,
There is nothing to fear.
The world is bad,
Situations are worst,
But...
Who cares,
When trust is there
When trust is there
Holding each other tight,
We always go right,
Promising to be with each other
Every day
And...
Every night,
Praying for things to be alright
To be alright.

For love is my religion
And you are my god,
My love for you is a never ending journey,
With shiny moon,
scary nights,
But also
With beautiful star,
Shinning bright.

XXI

ODE TO MY TEACHER

Imparting education, Nobility personified,
  Pulling young children out from the abyss of darkness
  Enlightening them through the rays of wisdom and knowledge;
  Mam, you are an epitome of elegance and positivity,
  Representing Naari Shakti to the core,
  Your confidence speaks a thousand words in itself
  Surrounding you with an aura of positivity and vibrance
  Showing children the world through your third Yogic eye
  Mam, you have contributed selflessly towards removing
  the growing menace of indifference and depravity amidst
humanity,
  For such is a true teacher- a nurturer, an educator
  Whose teachings go beyond the classroom lectures,
  Making students worldly-wise responsible citizens of the nation
  I salute your achievements in the field that you had chosen for
yourself,
  leaving behind perennial imprints of your success!
  May the Almighty always shower his benevalonce upon you.

XXII
ONE WINTER NIGHT

Walking on a road, one winter night,
Holding your hand damn so tight,
Looking at the moon, that shines so bright,
Those late night chats that we had,
Sometimes it makes me sad,
Though they are not so bad.
Yet, I remember that winter night
Holding your hand damn so tight.
Falling in love with your lovely eyes
Melting my heart from inside.
Still,
I remember those beautiful words,
That made me dance when I heard.
Falling for you, was not falling at all,
Excepting your proposal without thinking at all
You are my love after all
Every experience we must recall.
Walking on a road one winter night
Holding your hand damn so tight
Oh! My love let's take a flight
Struggle together to shine so bright
As together we are always right.

XXIII
OUT OF MANY FEARS

Smile on the face, Heart full of tears;
Living without a loved one is, one out of many fears.
Eyes are cold like the night in the winter,
Loneliness is chasing the soul like a hunter.
Even wealth of the whole world can't bring cheers,
Living without a loved one, is one out of many fears.
Winters without cold; and mind without you is impossible,
You make my soul dance, without youit can't be possible.
While walking beside you, the fog of the life clears,
Living without a loved one is, one out of many fears.
Leaves of life are covered with snow
My Lord! I wish to know!
Will ever the life be without snow?
May you never separate anybody's loved ones and dears,
Because living without a loved one is, one out of many fears.

ARTICLES & ANECDOTES

XXIV

DEALING WITH STRESS IN HARD TIMES

STRESS is a word that we all are familiar with, particularly 2020 has proved to be a very stressful year for the rich and the poor alike. The corona virus has brought the life to a standstill and everyone is facing stress in one way or the other. Now the question arises - how to manage stress? Is there any way to handle this problem? So here's the answer 'NO'-surprised? Of course you are surprised.

Let me clarify-

To quote a well known saying: ***"Every problem has a solution"***

But stress is not a problem. It's just a perception of mind created either in order to compete in the world or to succeed in the rat race or to shine all the above. When the situation turns upside down or against us, it is from where the stress enters. Actually we need to find out "Are we really stressed or we think that we are stressed. Almost every change in our lives whether it be an environmental, emotional, physical or even a pleasant change, it can cause stress. 'Yes' -even a pleasant change will put you in a stressful situation if your mind set and strategies are not correct to look upon or to accept the situation. Everything depends on us, solely on the choices made by us. Whenever you feel stressed just ask yourself once: 'are you really stressed?' If 'Yes' then ask and analyze 'Why'. Do you have any problem? And, here comes the first and the foremost step to cope up with stress is "Why Worry Theory" as explained by Gaur Gopal Das in his best seller **"Life's Amazing Secrets."** He says –

Ask yourself

Do you have a problem? If **'YES'** then ask 'Can you do something about it?' If **'YES'** then why worry ! And if the answer is **'NO'** then also 'why worry' because in that case you can't do anything . Then what is the benefit of worrying and taking stress? Why to give the remote of your mental peace into the hands of worry? Why to allow the outer situations rule and overpower our minds? By allowing them to rule we are giving an open invitation to so- called-stress, leading to the loss of mental stability.

Another strategy is to make a wise choice between looking at the world either from the problem-window or the solution-window. It is the game of choices that makes a difference. If we look from the problem-window, everything seems to be like a problem. Therefore leading to stress and then distress. But if we remain calm and composed and peep out through the solution-window, we will be able to create opportunities for ourselves even out of problematic situations. It purely depends on our action and reaction. The two divergent paths are right in front of us and it is in our hands to choose for ourselves. We ourselves are the best judges to change our mind-set, to change our life & to choose the best. Leave out the rest and don't stress.

Just remember nothing is permanent, so are these hard times. But let us not lose hopes.

We can certainly pray and hope for much better and peaceful days. And, with our positive approach, we are sure to see happier days ahead!!

XXV

Failure-A Brick in The Castle of Success

'Only those who dare to fail greatly can ever achieve greatly'.
– Robert F Kennedy

Failure is basically success turned inside out. It's an opportunity to explore a new possibility, it's a permission to discover something unknown and it's a chance to improve. But all this can only happen when we treat the concept of failure with the right attitude and work accordingly.

If we start seeing every failure as an opportunity and believe that we can make it to our goal, we are halfway there. At times we fear initiating a plan, we forget that what we must fear is not the failure but the chances that we will miss if we don't even try. There is literally nothing in nature that blooms all year long, so we must never expect ourselves to do so either; instead we should try to embrace our failures and imperfections because that's what makes success count. We need to understand that our only limit is our mind, once we go beyond that limit we can make our dreams come true. All we have is now, so our focus must be at the moment, spending our energies in moving forward towards our goal. Always remember that hardcore focus and alignment can put us years ahead in life, one must never underestimate the power of consistency and the desire of never giving up no matter how hard the path gets. Success should be seen as going from failure to failure without the loss of enthusiasm. Doubt kills more dreams than failure, never give up on what you desire the most, accept failures and setbacks but never accept not trying again. Never treat failure as the opposite of success instead look at it as a part of success. If success strikes the head then failure strikes the heart and gives success its flavor. Let your failures become your biggest inspirations. We all stumble and fall at times but it's only our comeback that makes it all matter. Whenever possible remind yourself that if you face failures don't step back, just begin again and this time a bit more rationally and intelligently. One must realize that success is not final, failure is not fatal, and it is the courage to continue that counts. Failure should never be treated as a defeat or as an end, how you overcome it matters the most.

As **J.K. Rowling** said – ***"It is impossible to live without failing at something, unless you live so cautiously that you might as well not have lived at all – in which case you fail by default."*** Just make sure you pursue your passion with so much devotion, that you no longer have time to fear failure. It all depends on your belief, if you believe that it will work out, you will see opportunities but if your belief says it won't then you will see obstacles. No one ever said that success would come easy, one must be willing to fall over and over again in order to taste success. Failure improves you as a person and makes you understand the importance of struggle. We as humans are allowed to model the strength and courage that comeback takes. Our situation never defines us, how we overcome it does. Once you start fighting failures you will love the process. Just be unstoppable and keep growing despite the failures or doubts. Persistence and effort should be the key as they can change failures into extraordinary achievements. Never think of failure as a loss instead think of it as a gain which lets you change and grow. Every shooting star is a proof that falling can be beautiful, when you give in your all. Our mindset is very powerful, it can make us or break us, and all we need is to fight a strong battle through some bad days to earn the best days of our life. We all need to train ourselves in a way that we stop avoiding failures because success never comes from avoiding the pain in a hope for the gain. Difficult roads often lead to beautiful destinations, the path is tough but so are you and that is where the power lies. No matter how many defeats you encounter but you must not be defeated by any. Everything you have ever wanted is on the other side of the fear, so one must not fear any failures and setbacks, they are just a part of one's success and growth. At last we all must remember that a winner is a dreamer who never gave up so keep trying until you succeed.

As it is famously said that ***"Either a person wins or the person learns"***, this collection of works aims at depicting the undying spirit of some individuals who treated failure in the way it should be and turned the tide in their favor.

XXVI
CORONA TIME: BLESSING IN DISGUIDE

Change is the only constant. Never before has this saying scenes more truth then in this current times. As truly said – **"There is success in every failure; a new learning guards your further steps. The glass is half filled; optimism glows your personality."**

It's all about perspective in which way we direct our minds.

The Corona scared and now the lockdown... it is like a nightmare. People are suffering and dying across the world. There is even a sense of guilt for having the luxury delivered at our doorstep. The situation resulting in the loss of courage and the negativity surrounds from every nuke and corner.

Remember,**"It's our attitude at the beginning of a difficult task or situation which more than anything else, will affect the successful outcome."**

The entire world is grappling with a pandemic that has brought about monumental change in the very way of life. From workplace to Marketplace and specially the educational scenario. Nothing has undergone as tremendous change as the education system. From congregating classrooms to attending the classes online, students have had to bring about a great change in their study method. Weather this change is for better or worse is a matter of perspective. Though this lockdown has kept us inside our home but at the same time it has been a blessing in disguise in a bigger picture. For instance, it has given us a great opportunity to slow down, analyse and introspect ourselves to find out shortcomings and work on them. The big advantage of this period is that it has given us time to work on ourselves psychologically. This is where all the online learning platforms have come to our rescue and during this time the scope of online learning is much larger than ever before. Earlier online learning was limited only to a few web portals which provide limited and costly content but due to the lock down all the skilled people including teachers, musicians, chefs, artists etc. have come up with countless online learning courses which provide top notch content at an affordable costs.

Online teaching in context of school and college students has helped to keep up their curriculum from the safety and comfort of their home. Hence ensuring that their study is not compromised. Further, it opens up new endeavours to gain more and more proficiency and command over the subject for teachers, parents as well as students.

As we all know that every situation have advantages and disadvantages attached to it, thus Corona situation is not an exception. Therefore we have some shortcomings also such as online learning requires more time than on-campus classes, it may create sense of isolation, allows more independence, sometimes there are less availability of courses, connectivity issues mostly hamper the online learning as well as teaching but these issues are temporary which will be solved which time and experience as we get used to the concept. Therefore, **"Just don't give up trying to do what you really want to do."**

With this spirit we can turn the pandemic time into a blessing in disguise.

XXVII
BACK TO NATURE

A peaceful afternoon nap is one of the things I enjoy the most in life. I have never had a more peaceful nap than when I was a child and used to sleep under the cool shade of a tree surrounded by lush green fields. The fast-paced life of the city has given me much but it could never provide me that carefree afternoon nap that I had as a child. Now, the corona virus has ripped through my well-established city routine like a hurricane and while locked inside the comfort of my plush house, I long to be surrounded by those gigantic banyan trees and flowing rice fields.

I look at the huge towers and buildings surrounding me and imagine how many bamboo, banyan or teak trees must have been chopped down to build these gilded cages. We ooh and ahh at the colossal skyscrapers and become mesmerized by the gigantic shopping malls but we have forgotten how enthralling it was like to climb atop that huge coconut tree and shake-off those water and *malai* filled coconuts. In ancient times nature, especially trees used to be worshipped like gods. But now the human footprint has become so large that to accommodate it trees are cut-down, lakes are drained, oceans are pushed back, air is polluted and flora and fauna are sacrificed. The corona virus is a slap in the face of mankind to awaken us from our slumber and reflect on the devastation we have wrought on this planet to satisfy our selfish desires.

William Wordsworth famously said, **"Come forth into the light of things, let nature be your teacher."** It is high time that humans returned to the lap of nature for it is in nature that we can find the secret to living that enriched and fulfilling life that we desire. Nature can be the best teacher only if the student knows where to look.

The earth teaches us patience and endurance, water teaches us to overcome any obstacle, air teaches us purity that is unaffected by good or bad and sun teaches us to treat everyone alike without any discrimination. Every lesson of life can be found in nature but sadly we have completely disconnected ourselves from natural life and become immersed in the latest technology. Instead of trying to preserve the bounty of nature we have become the biggest perpetrators of its destruction. Due to man's greed and unabated scientific and technological advancement the planet has become unfit for sustaining life. According to a 2015 study, nearly five hundred species of animals and birds have gone extinct since 1900, out of which ten have gone extinct in the last decade alone.

The survival of mankind is hanging by a thread. The largest metropolitan cities in the world are a breeding ground for a number of physiological diseases and the stressful fast paced life gives rise to tremendous mental strain. Our earth is pleading:

"Save me! Save me

I shout and scream

But,

There is no one to come forward and clean,

Everyone is busy in their dreams,

I am dying day by day,

While saving your pride in every way

Save me for I am becoming dry and grey,

Otherwise...

Your future generations will cry

And,

You will die in a deep sigh."

It is now paramount to limit the use and advancement of technology and to go back to a simpler but more enriching lifestyle. The corona virus pandemic has taught us that we should be wise enough to know when to stop.

As the technology driven world decreased its pace, nature bloomed. Air quality improved, the water bodies became waste-free. Birds not seen for years were seen flying about and man has learnt to take a step back and just breathe.

It is sad that it took a pandemic and the loss of many lives for us to stop our mad rat race. There is still time to learn and stop our destructive activities and preserve nature so that someday our future generations can also take a relaxing nap under the cool shade of some tree.

Nature has set the reset button for us, now it is up to us to shape the future of this planet.

XXVIII
HOPE

"It is not about the destination, but the journey"

This is one of the sayings that I have lived by in the last 26 years of my life. An individual faces several challenges and situations in life and at times they weigh more than the individual can carry. During those times, it is very easy to give up and just let things be the way they are. Picking up the sword seems more difficult as compared to picking up the spirits, not leaving the comfort zone seems easier than leaving the habits that have got us to the challenging situation. Everything seems dark, dusky, and worthless. That is the time when one of the strongest emotions known to mankind comes into play which has time and again proved why is it called so. It's a four-letter word but has the ability to do wonders for an individual from all four directions – HOPE. Obvious it might seem, but actually, it is not so simple. We, in our daily life always fail to fathom the magnanimous potential of this emotion. Hope actually has a full form that openly explains the meaning behind the emotion.

HOPE- Have Only Positive Expectations

It is not about just daydreaming about all the positive things that you think can happen in your life. It is much more than that. Whenever there are challenges in life and they start taking the best of you, Hope is one of the things that has the ability to give you that extra boost of motivation that will keep you in the game. Situations and challenges might be able to put you down but with the hope, they won't be able to push you out of the game. But just like all things in this world, hope also has some basic requirements and features. Firstly, it does not come just by thinking and expecting positive things. If that were the case then it would have been very easy for almost everybody to do so. But we all know it does not work that way. It starts with the realization that there are things that will not go the way we planned or the way we thought about them and it is absolutely normal. As it is said very famously in the military setups that no plan survives the first contact with the enemy, it is true in life as well. So the moral is that one has to be ready for a change in actions, change in plans, and change in outlook. Most of the plans that we work out are mere directions that we set up for ourselves to streamline our approach. It may or may not work out the way we have thought. There is a power above all that controls the universe and all that happens to each individual. Once the realization is there the second step is the readiness to put in the effort. Again, there is a famous quote that says,

"Life is all about how you handle your plan B"

It is so true to its core. Generally, we are so obsessed with the splendor of our mega PLAN A that we forget to prepare about the reverse situation. Always be ready to put the effort into PLAN B. This reduces the mental pressure that clouds one's judgment when Plan A is set to fall. When we fail in our top plan, it is generally not the fear or sorrow of failing that troubles us but instead, it is the sense of loss of future direction that strikes a lightning stroke of fear in our mind and soul. In such situations, we feel that now there is nothing we can do, and to start a new plan or retry the first plan, a long journey would have to be taken again. In such conditions, the pressure on the head is so high and since in today's world the negative influences are abundant, it is inevitable that most of us get entangled in the vicious cycle of negativity. Hence having a plan B goes a long way in easing out the steam and thinking rationally.

The third and the most important component in my opinion is something that everybody knows about but most don't understand. It's called self-confidence. If a person has self-confidence, it has the capability to bypass all the above-mentioned requirements and keep a person motivated all through the voyages of our lives. Self-confidence is that power bank, that nitrous booster (young minds can relate), and that reservoir of positivity and inner belief that keeps everyone in the games of respective lives. It is easy to feel motivated and invincible when the situations are conducive. But the real test of one's self-confidence is when things are in the opposite directions and the chances of recovery are low. To build self-confidence is like a daily "sadhana" that any individual has to do. It builds up slowly but once it is complete, it becomes an invincible fort. Self-confidence is not something that one gets by genes. Instead, it has to be built from the bottom up. Yes to a good extent the upbringing of an individual is one of the deciding factors in this regard (that's why it is important to promote and impart such qualities in our younger generation rather than only bookish and in-trend ones), but it is extremely important to build the self-confidence all through one's life. It is totally dependent on the effort one puts in his or her life. Qualities like readiness to learn new things and putting in the effort to explore new areas and aspects of life, reading, socializing, and working on one's personal aspects like physical fitness, general and social awareness, etc. help a lot in increasing one's confidence.

Well, it is not like I am sharing all this from my imagination only. I have personally gone through a funny journey in my life which has given me the chance to learn the above lessons. Being from a family of educationists, there was always pressure to do well academically which was not natural to me. Though I was a vibrant, outspoken person involved in sports, music, debates, and other activities, I was not able to do that well academically despite my best efforts, and also the loss of certain family members pushed me into darkness. That was my meeting with depression which took its toll on all aspects of life and kept me there for around two years.

Having taken the extreme step and spending the prime time of my life alone, in dark closed rooms was something that I wish nobody ever has to face. But then there were positive influences in the form of people, movies, and books that started a recovery phase. I started doing martial arts and as my physicality grew stronger, it helped open up my mind. I excelled in the same and won belts and medals including at the national level. I fell in love with geopolitics and world affairs and that opened my vision totally. Also, my love for music was assisting me. I made a comeback and learned about the power of hope. I aimed at joining the Indian army which was my plan A and for me, it was a redemption of the past shortcomings. Also, I had worked very hard for the same, going for workouts at 5 AM winter mornings and doing the same late at night; meeting people, participating in debates and discussions, reading a lot, following current affairs, etc. all along with my B-tech. The journey started in 2015 and everything was so conducive and hence uplifting. But in 2018 I was diagnosed with a medical problem that turned the tables. Recovery needed 1 year and when the year passed, in came the COVID-19. In 2021 the process started again but I got Covid due to which I couldn't appear. Now, I am overage for the same. So after seven years and sixteen failed attempts, my Plan A ended after giving me nothing. I was at square one- grass root level. But all these years taught me how to deal with this. My Plan B was entrepreneurship which I am perusing now and I run 3 companies side by side and have plans to launch my 4th venture in the coming months. I am handling my PLAN B. I am still into music, geopolitics, and world affairs and living a satisfying life. Now I am an individual who is literally unbreakable and come what may, I know I am capable of doing anything, irrespective of my past.

So folks don't overburden yourself with what has not gone your way. Look forward. If hope worked for an average person like me, it will surely work wonders for you all highly capable ones.

Stay strong, enjoy life, and wear a smile. Always.

XXIX

Professeure virtual versus reel (Virtual versus Real Teacher)

Teaching is the art of bringing out the human in a human being. It is not just merely a profession; it's the bedrock of the future of generations. The way in which a whole generation is taught in the formative years, is the prime deciding factor of the future of a society. Traditional teaching methodology has been tried and tested over the years and have given us good results. But now the times have changed. The reach of education is deeper, the number of students is higher, and the curriculum is diverse and informative. Today's students are much more active, informed, clever and dynamic in nature. The introduction of technology in the form of internet, social media, television and other gadgetry, the information scope of today's students is vast and the ability of these technological devices to influence the students is immense. Unfortunately, our teaching and learning methods have not been able to develop at the same speed and cope up with the changing times. Along with technological development, traditional teaching methods have been challenged by various technologically enhanced teaching and learning methods. This trend has received mixed reactions: On one hand it is apprehensive that these new technologies will replace teachers altogether. On the other hand, the expectations towards technology can also be over-optimistic; that it will solve all the problems of learning. The use of technology changes the role of the teacher from a traditional knowledge provider to a facilitator, guiding the students' learning process and engages in problem-solving with them. In addition, technology offers a range of new types of learning possibilities also.

Such as in medieval times, books were rare and only the elite had access to educational opportunities. Individuals had to travel to centers of learning to get educated. But today, massive amounts of information (books, audio, images, videos) are available at one's fingertips through the Internet, and the opportunities of formal learning are available online worldwide through MOOCs, podcasts, traditional online degree programs, and more. Access to learning opportunities in the present times is very easy. Thanks to technology that now everyone can learn being at their home or office place not only this but a learner can choose his or her suitable times also as most of these courses are self-paced.

These advancements have made the situation very easy, reachable and affordable too. But there is a big doubt on the whole concept of e-learning or online learning, that is weather these new learning concepts are really that effective when it comes to parting not only information but real knowledge? Are these systems ready to replace traditional methods? Are these systems fool-proof? All these systems capable of replacing a traditional teacher in the learning and teaching sphere?

These are some questions that have come up into lime light in the backdrop of the COVID-19 pandemic which has resulted in the shutting down of almost all small and big educational institutions and has caged us in our homes. This question is like weather a calculator can replace a mathematics teacher at work? There are several versions of the answer to this question but the average answer is a no. As truly said:

"It's the teacher that makes difference, not the classroom."

Technology by no means can be a replacement for teachers, but yes, it can be used effectively to enhance the learning process. Many schools, all across the world, today, have incorporated the advancements brought up by the technology such as incorporation of smart classes, access of e-content etc. to ease the learning process for students. It helps the teachers to easily teach the most difficult of concepts using the graphics and animations from the repository. Moreover, the students also get better and quicker understanding of the subjects. Technology changes the way we access information, but also how we're taught that information. The instructor becomes less of a 'sage on stage' and more of a 'guide on the side.' From accessing course materials online to watching video-recorded lectures, technology opens up the possibility for teaching innovation: from collaborative group work to flipped and hybrid classrooms. Instructors can also use classroom response systems to assess students' understanding of course material and adjust the pace or content as needed in real time. While technology is sometimes seen as a threat—and it does have its limits—integrating it into your teaching practice offers a new way for students to interact and engage with course material. Thanks to technology, education is no longer confined to the walls of your classroom. YouTube videos and social media don't have to be a distraction; they can be part of your course material. The math is easy: it adds up to better learning outcomes.

But everything is possible only if we have someone to guide. Therefore we may conclude that though technology opens up many doors for learning but it cannot replace a teacher because it is a teacher who guides a learner to attain maximum benefits.

"It is important to remember that educational software is only one tool in the learning process. Neither can be a substitute for well-trained teachers, leadership, and parental involvement." – Keith Krueger

XXX

Melt the Stress, Heal the mind!

Overthinking – You can't control everything, Just let it be!

Thoughts surely are powerful. Whatever we hold on in our mind for long, reflects in our really life. Stress or overthinking can be best defined as – thinking too much about something or for too long. It happens with all of us at some point of time in our lives – we all experience stressful events that make us worry more. But some people can't turn off their concerns no matter how hard they try. They tend to worry endlessly about the future, make catastrophic predictions about the events that never happened and are easily disturbed by uncertainty. Stress or overthinking is psychologically harmful because the mind replays the negative experiences in an endless loop that can cause emotional distress. We all need to breathe and understand this simple fact that this loss of control over thoughts is the major cause of our sadness and despair. We need to keep our mind off things that aren't helping us. Remember, when you can't control what goes around,

JUST BREATHE!

Stress involves a form of fear which tends to get worse by adding anticipations, uncertainty, imagination and emotions to it. It can ruin you, confuse you, twist things around and make everything seem much worse than it actually is. There is nothing in this world that can trouble you as much as your own thoughts, so stop stressing over things you can't control. One should never let the fear of past and uncertainty of the future ruin the happiness of their present. Almost everything will work again if you unplug it for a few minutes, *Including You!* .Stress is caused by being 'Here' but wanting to be 'There'. If it is out of your hands it deserves freedom from your mind too. Don't believe in every worried thought you have, worried thoughts are notoriously inaccurate. Stress is always caused by your thoughts, not the situation and it is perfectly okay to admit that you need time. Just stop trying to run on an empty tank. Remember you can do anything but not everything. You don't have to control your thoughts, you just have to stop letting them control you. A negative mind will never give you a positive life. Some days you will feel like the ocean, some days you will feel like you are drowning in it. Nothing is permanent, no matter how bad the situation is it will change, you just need to stop worrying over it. You're not going to master the rest of your life in one day, just relax and master the day then just keep doing that every day. Your calm mind is the ultimate weapon against your challenges, So Relax. An empty lantern provides no light, *Self Care* is the fuel that allows your light to shine brightly. Self Care is the new Health Care. Just when you feel that you have no time to relax, know that this is the moment when you need to make time to relax.

5 simple Mantras for eliminating Stress!!

Mantra 1 – I will not hesitate, I will just do what I need to do.

Mantra 2 – I will accept what I cannot control.

Mantra 3 – With every Deep Breath I take, I feel myself becoming calmer.

Mantra 4 – I accept myself as I am.

Mantra 5 – I've done more than enough today.

The body achieves what the mind believes!!

Overthinking or Stress is an issue of national concern among young and middle aged adults but is relatively less common among older adults. It also contributes to severe Depression and Anxiety plus interferes with the daily functioning. Research indicates that 57% of women and 43% of men are overthinkers. The ones who tend to overthink are more likely to abuse drugs and alcohol and it may even push some individuals to consider or attempt suicide.

This is tough, but so are you! You weren't born an over thinker – we all have specific behavior and thought patterns which are learned over time through experiences and just as they are learned they can also be unlearned. The key to identify what causes you to overthink and how you can manage those triggers. It all lies within you and if you have the determination to "stop" this, you may keep in mind certain points:-

- Acknowledge your fears and try to accept them.
- Practice self – compassion and be kind to yourself.
- Let go off perfection, strive for "good enough" rather than perfect.
- Embrace mistakes as they are a part of self growth.
- Stay present focused; don't spend your time in "what if land".
- Learn to relax your mind and body with activities such as meditation, exercise, listening to soothing music, massage and aroma therapy.

Once you discover how to stop stressing and living in the moment you'll be happier. Always remember that life happens for you, not to you. Sometimes 'It is OK to not be Okay'. Just be selective with your battles, at times peace is better than being right.

If ocean can calm itself, so can you!